Evil Brain Chips

Written by Jonny Zucker
Illustrated by Ian Tovey

Titles in Full Flight Fear & Fun

Space Plague   Skyrunners
Bubble Attack   Spook Manor
Circus Scam   Dark Detective
Evil Brain Chips   Valley of Wisdom
Football Killers   Maxi Beasts

Badger Publishing Limited
Oldmedow Road, Hardwick Industrial Estate,
King's Lynn PE30 4JJ
Telephone: 01438 791037
www.badgerlearning.co.uk

2 4 6 8 10 9 7 5 3 1

Evil Brain Chips   ISBN 978 1 84691 127 9

First edition © 2007
This second edition © 2013

Text © Jonny Zucker 2007
Complete work © Badger Publishing Limited 2007

All rights reserved. No part of this publication may be
reproduced, stored in any form or by any means mechanical,
electronic, recording or otherwise without
the prior permission of the publisher.

The right of Jonny Zucker to be identified as author of
this Work has been asserted by him in accordance with
the Copyright, Designs and Patents Act 1988.

Series Editor: Jonny Zucker
Publisher: David Jamieson
Commissioning Editor: Carrie Lewis
Editor: Paul Martin
Design: Fiona Grant
Illustration: Ian Tovey

Evil Brain Chips

Contents

1. The Smash — 5
2. On the Run — 9
3. Hooking Up — 13
4. Up and Out — 19
5. Face the Enemy — 23
6. Brain Free — 27

It is the year 2265.

At birth, every baby has a microchip put into their brain. This lets the evil President Fader control every person with his special control panel. He also controls the evil Police Crew.

But the day Kris Jenson was born, the microchip machine broke down. So Kris has no chip in his brain. He is a 'Free One'.

Kris has found one other Free One – a very old scientist called the Doc. Together they are working in a lab – on a top-secret project.

That project is nearly ready.

1. The Smash

It was late. The Doc and Kris were very, very tired. They had been working non-stop for 24 hours.

They locked up the lab and hurried back to the Doc's flat. It was a very windy night. In the distance they could hear the sirens of Police Crew vans.

It took them ten minutes to get back to the Doc's flat. The Doc pressed a code on the wall panel and the door to his flat slid open.

Just then the doorbell rang. Answering the door in this city could be dangerous.

Before Kris could look at the door camera, the windows were smashed in and glass flew all over the Doc's flat.

2. On the Run

The Police Crew marched in with stun guns and batons.

The Police Crew drew their stun guns and fired at Kris. Stun pellets flew through the air and smashed into the walls. But he was too quick for them.

The rubbish hatch led out onto a flat roof. Kris sped across it with the Police Crew right behind him. He knew he could not slip up. Any slip could mean death.

Come back here! You cannot get away from us!

Where to now?

At the edge of the roof was a massive drop. Kris had two choices: he could either stand there and wait for the Police Crew to catch him or... jump for it.

3. Hooking Up

Kris was inside an office. He was face-to-face with a boy his own age.

The boys made it to the underground train station very quickly.

The boys sped down the tunnel. very cold and they could hear of their footsteps. Rats ran alo tracks and spiders' webs hung from the walls.

How far away is the way into Fader's palace?

There is a door about half a mile away.

But then a sharp beam of light
appeared ahead and the boys heard a
rumbling sound.

You said we had ten minutes! We have only been in here for five.

It's my watch! It must have stopped when I jumped into that office.

There was no way out. The train was
heading for them at 100 miles per
hour. They would be crushed to death.

4. Up and Out

The train was only seconds away.

Kris and Otto found a long metal ladder. It led up a shaft. There was a thin circle of light at the top.

The boys tiptoed down a narrow corridor. There were grey doors on either side. They could hear the clank and buzz of machines through the doors.

Let's check out that door over there.

Kris pushed the door open. But someone was waiting on the other side.

This is not the welcome we were hoping for.

5. Face the Enemy

The Police Crew pushed their guns into the boys' backs.

The Police Crew pushed the boys into a room. They were amazed by what they saw.

A door creaked open and the boys heard footsteps. Was it more Police Crew, or was it something even worse?

Welcome to my little factory. I am so glad you could pop in for a visit.

This is not a visit. We have come to stop you!

6. Brain Free

Otto grabbed a metal trolley and slammed it backwards as hard as he could.

Kris grabbed the President's control panel. Now he could control everyone with a microchip in their brain – and that included the Police Crew!

Kris told Fader to stay in the storeroom. Fader did what he was told.